pray with me

A thirty day prayer journey as a couple.

Dan and Rebekah Metteer

Published by Loving The Leap Ministries
© 2018 Dan and Rebekah Metteer
lovingtheleapministries@gmail.com

Designed by Sara Marie Qualls
sara.marie.qualls@gmail.com

Printed in the United States of America.

DEDICATION

This book is dedicated to our kids
Julia, Katie, & Andrew.

Our desire is that, through our example,
you will witness the value of prayer,
and that one day,
you will each make it a priority
to pray with your spouse.

START HERE

WELCOME to your 30 day prayer journey as a couple. We trust that the Lord will amaze you with his peace, provision, and miracles as you agree together in prayer. We hope you will be strengthened in your relationship as you release your cares to God.

START BY SETTING A SPECIFIC TIME AND PLACE. Morning works best for us, even though we are both NOT morning people. We find that starting the day with prayer sets the tone for all that we set out to do. Choose a convenient place that takes little effort to arrive at. For us, it is the couch closest to our room. Sometimes, we even have to move the laundry over in order to find a place to sit.

BE CONSISTENT. Your prayer time does not need to be long, just consistent. We pray together each morning before our kids get out of bed at 6:30 a.m. on our living room sofa. Just being present with an open heart is all that is needed.

ALTERNATE READING DAYS. Husbands will read the odd numbered days, and wives will read the even numbered days. Each day begins with a personalized scripture. Read the scripture twice, once read by the husband for the wife, and a second time from the wife over the husband. Take turns reading the devotionals on your odd or even numbered days. At the end of the devotional, take a moment to ask each other three specific things that you would like prayer about and write them in the space provided.

PRAY OUT LOUD. After you have filled in your requests, husband & wife will take turns reading the written prayer provided, and end it by adding on the prayer requests that each of you have requested prayer for.

GUIDELINES FOR PRAYING TOGETHER

1. After reading the scripture and devotional, end by asking, "How can I pray for you today?"

2. Write down three specific requests that your husband or wife has given.

3. Keep your requests personal to you or your day/week ahead. Try to avoid praying for third party requests or other people's needs unless that person or circumstance is specifically affecting your life (such as your children's needs, etc.). This is a great time to allow your spouse to "know you" a little bit better and the things that are weighing on your heart. Trust each other enough to open up.

4. Avoid solving your partner's problems during your prayer time together. This is a time to listen and to bring his or her need before the One who has the ability to fix it. This isn't even the time to ask a lot of questions about your spouse's request. Just bring it to the Lord.

5. Do your best not to "preach" at your spouse in your prayer, but rather, talk directly to God without adding in your own judgment or opinion to the prayer.

6. Talk to God like you would talk to a friend. No need for fancy words, just sincere hearts. But DO be aware that your prayers are changing things!

A NOTE ON PERSONALIZED SCRIPTURES

We believe that the Word of God is infallible and should not be added to or taken away from. However, adding in your spouse's name to a Bible verse, as we have done on most days, is an exercise of principle. It is not meant to be a substitute for the context of scripture, but rather to help you apply scripture to your life and to be thinking about its truths throughout the day. Certainly, not all scripture can be replaced with your own name, but we chose verses that we believe have principles that would apply to any life. We also believe there is power in speaking God's truths over your life, and we are excited for you to declare these things for one another.

HOW TO USE THIS BOOK IN A NUTSHELL

1. Pick a specific time and place to pray together for 10 or 15 minutes and stick with it.

2. Husband, start by praying the personalized scripture over your wife.

3. Wife, repeat the scripture at the top of each day, personalizing it with your husband's name.

4. Husband will read the odd numbered days' devotions.

5. Wife will read the even numbered days' devotions.

6. Each take a moment to ask, "How can I pray for you?" Write down three personal prayer requests.

7. Husband, end by reading the personalized written prayer over your wife and adding her 3 requests to that prayer.

8. Wife, finish by reading the personalized written prayer over your husband and adding his 3 requests to that prayer.

9. Repeat this pattern for 30 days. For reference, we usually pray together 5 days a week, as Saturday and Sunday carry a unique timeline for us.

TABLE OF CONTENTS

Husband & Wife, each take a turn reading the verse below out loud as a way of speaking blessing over your spouse. Personalize the verse with your husband's or wife's name. Read it twice so that both names are read.

"Each time he said, 'My grace is all_____ need[s]. My power works best in weakness'...For when [he/she] is weak, then [he/she] is strong" II Cor. 12:9a, 10b.

{ DAY 1 STRENGTH }

HUSBAND READS:

Strength seems like it is in short supply. Life is a challenging venture, and when looking around at the world and thinking about what needs to be done, one immediately begins to think, "I am too tired, too overwhelmed, too strapped for time, and too weak to meet the demands before me." When we do find the strength to try to overcome our challenges, we quickly tire. There never seems to be enough strength to cover everything.

But strength looks different for the servants of God. Our weakness does not make us less qualified for the tasks of life. Instead, our weakness makes space for his strength. The more we realize that we cannot meet our most real needs, the more we can turn our expectation to him--the God of all strength--to meet the needs before us. When we know we are weak, we allow him to demonstrate his strength.

God does not leave us weak. He becomes our strength so that our identity is no longer that we are tired, weak, and overwhelmed. By his strength we become strong. We run without growing weary--we soar on wings like eagles (Isaiah 40:31).

HUSBAND & WIFE, take a moment now to ask each other, "How can I pray for you today?" Then write down those three requests in the space provided below. After you've written the requests, read the prayers below and add your spouse's three requests to your prayer.

HUSBAND PRAYS FOR WIFE:

Heavenly Father, be with _____ today. Let her rest in your strength. Where she feels tired, let her see how you are working and fighting on her behalf. Where she is weak, make her know that you are strong in her, and that you have made her strong because of your mighty power. I also pray for. . .

1 _____

2 _____

3 _____

WIFE PRAYS FOR HUSBAND:

Lord, lead _____ with your power. Be his strength today so that he can overcome every challenge that he will face. Let him learn to admit and embrace his own weakness so that you can be made even stronger in his life. I also pray for . . .

1 _____

2 _____

3 _____

strength

Husband & Wife, each take a turn reading the verse below out loud as a way of speaking blessing over your spouse. Personalize the verse with your husband's or wife's name. Read it twice so that both names are read.

"May the God of hope fill_____with all joy and peace in believing, so that by the power of the Holy Spirit_____may abound in hope" Romans 15:13.

{ DAY 2 }
JOY

WIFE READS:

What an incredible thought--that God desires to continuously pour out his joy into each of us until we are completely full--100% satisfied with our joy level. How is your joy level? If you are unsatisfied with it, there is a key in the verse above. The key is belief. Believing that God's power is complete, that his authority is supreme, that his ability is beyond, and that this is the God who dwells in you with the day ahead, the stresses real, and the unknowns looming.

When we ask the Lord to give us joy, we often view it like a spoonful of sugar, as if a little bit of joy would momentarily mask the joyless part of a life that is desperately choking down reality. But what if this God-given joy--with its potent, fragrant, powerful consistency--had the ability to fill that cup from the bottom up and push out joylessness until all hopeless thoughts were left on the saucer?

It's a wonderful gift to be filled with joy, and this is what God promises to do as we put our belief in him. And yet, would a measure of joy even change your circumstances today? Perhaps not. But it would lift your spirit! It would give you energy as you rest in the strength of God to take care of the things which you cannot control. Joy is not just a bright and cheery notion that one has in fields of flowers. Joy is not just for parties and pageants. It's for illuminating dark places, and defeating depression. It is a powerful work against the enemy who would love to crush your spirit and drag you down.

When I think about joy, I often think about light and warmth breaking through a gray and darkened day. There's an old song that says, "Turn your eyes upon Jesus. Look full in his wonderful face, and the things of earth will grow strangely dim in the light of his glory and grace." Joy is the light your spirit needs to press into the day ahead with greater hope than yesterday. As we look to the radiance of God's glory, his ability, and his power, and as we believe deep in our hearts that he IS over all things, we are filled with joy, security, and hope.

HUSBAND & WIFE, take a moment now to ask each other, "How can I pray for you today?" Then write down those three requests in the space provided below. After you've written the requests, read the prayers below and add your spouse's three requests to your prayer.

WIFE PRAYS FOR HUSBAND:

Dear Lord, I pray for_____today that joy would push out every joyless place in his heart, mind, and soul. In every circumstance_____faces, I pray that the truth of who you are would fill him with unexplainable joy. I pray that joy would be the weapon that makes the lies of the enemy disappear in Jesus' name. I also pray for...

1 _____

2 _____

3 _____

HUSBAND PRAYS FOR WIFE:

Lord, I pray for_____. I pray that you would fill her up with great joy today. I pray that she would believe you, have hope in you, and that you would give her peace as she rests in your great love. I also pray for...

1

2

_____

3

_____

_____

joy

Husband & Wife, each take a turn reading the verse below out loud as a way of speaking blessing over your spouse.

"The Lord God said, 'It is not good for the man to be alone. I will make a helper suitable for him.'" Genesis 2:18.

{ DAY 3 }
FRIENDSHIP

HUSBAND READS:

Friendship is central to who we are as humans. We yearn for friendship in the same way we yearn for sunlight or even food. We need it.

Husbands and wives may not always think of their marriage as a friendship, but, in reality, your marriage should be the closest friendship that you ever have. The very first friendship--Adam and Eve--was a marriage. God created them specifically for companionship with each other.

All friendships, though, are friendships "about" something. When you were young, you were probably friends with someone because you both lived on the same street--your friendship was about living near each other. Or later, you may have been friends with some people because you were in the same class at school with them, or because of a sport you both played, or an activity that you both enjoyed. But when the things you have in common fade away, the friendship usually doesn't last.

Many marriages fail because the couple forgets that they are supposed to be friends. A marriage relationship needs to be about something. That is why communication, dedicated interest in each other, shared experiences, and common goals are so important. But, at its core, every marriage should be about Jesus. Anything else that a friendship could be about will eventually fade away, but Jesus never will. And he is the one who made you, the one who saved you from sin, the one who ordained your marriage, and the one who knows both you and your spouse better than anyone. When your marriage is about him, your friendship with your spouse will be deep, satisfying, and unshakeable.

HUSBAND & WIFE, take a moment now to ask each other, "How can I pray for you today?" Then write down those three requests in the space provided below. After you've written the requests, read the prayers below and add your spouse's three requests to your prayer.

HUSBAND PRAYS FOR WIFE:

Jesus, thank you for bringing_____and me together. I pray that our relationship would be *about* you. Help us to follow your Spirit's leading in our communication, our present circumstances, and our future. I also pray for . . .

1 _____

2 _____

3 _____

WIFE PRAYS FOR HUSBAND:

Lord, bless the friendship between_____ and me. Knit us together in a way that honors you. Show us how you want to be the center of our relationship. I also pray for. . .

1 _____

2 _____

3 _____

friendship

Husband & Wife, each take a turn reading the verse below out loud as a way of speaking blessing over your spouse. Personalize the verse with your husband's or wife's name. Read it twice so that both names are read.

"Then_____will discern the fear of the Lord and discover the knowledge of God. For the Lord gives wisdom; from His mouth comes knowledge and understanding. He stores up sound wisdom for the upright; He is a shield to those who walk in integrity" Proverbs 2:5-6.

{ DAY 4 WISDOM }

WIFE READS:

Wisdom is the current that propels you to understanding. Wisdom is the vision corrector that gives you clear sight for the will of God. Wisdom is the character shaper that chisels away the longing for self-fulfillment and leaves you as a vessel willing to be used by God.

The Lord is offering us a gift called wisdom. When you receive it, you are suddenly aware of your own inability to solve the issues at hand. Wisdom recognizes the frailty of self and bows its knee to the omniscient knowledge of God. Take a second to think of the things that are in front of you, all the questions and unknown decisions that must be made. You are at a crossroads. Fear, self-doubt, and self-sufficiency on the left, and surrender, humility, and a quest for wisdom on the right. Today, if you ask for wisdom, God is willing to direct you toward his will. He will show you where to step. He will direct you when to stop. He will prompt your heart to speak, or cause you to hold your tongue.

You are serving a trustworthy God who knows what the outcome of your future is. He has good plans, as it mentions in Jeremiah 29:11. Proverbs 2:5-6 says that God is storing up sound wisdom for you as you walk in obedience to him. In what ways can you tune your heart to his voice today? In what areas can you bend your actions toward obedience and faith? Allow the true prayer of your heart to long for wisdom, which is the laying down of self, and the determined quest for the will of God to be accomplished. God gives this wisdom freely, but self-sufficiency must be fought in order to desire God's good, pleasing, and perfect will. Open up your hand and ask for wisdom to discern what He already knows is best for you.

HUSBAND & WIFE, take a moment now to ask each other, "How can I pray for you today?" Then write down those three requests in the space provided below. After you've written the requests, read the prayers below and add your spouse's three requests to your prayer.

WIFE PRAYS FOR HUSBAND:

Jesus, I pray for_____today. I pray that when he asks you for wisdom, you would supernaturally give it to him. I pray that_____would discover YOU today and that his heart would be filled with joy, peace, and security knowing that you are directing him in the way he should go. Bless him in all that he does. I also pray for...

1 _____

2 _____

3 _____

HUSBAND PRAYS FOR WIFE:

Lord, I pray for_____in all the decisions she needs to make. Give her wisdom that comes from your Holy Spirit. Grant her discernment and strength as she faces challenges. I also pray for ...

1 _____

2 _____

3 _____

wisdom

Husband & Wife, each take a turn reading the verse below out loud as a way of speaking blessing over your spouse. Personalize the verse with your husband's or wife's name. Read it twice so that both names are read.

"Do not be afraid. Stand firm and_____ will see the deliverance the Lord will bring [him/her] today...The Lord will fight for_____; [he/she] need only to be still" Exodus 14:13-14.

{ DAY 5
FEAR }

HUSBAND READS:

It would not be difficult to make a list of one-hundred things that you could be afraid of--things that could trip you up, cause you permanent harm, or even destroy you. And while many of those things will never happen, it is still possible for your mind to be overwhelmed with legitimate fear. Fear is real, and the things that we are afraid of can be real too.

But for those who are under the protection of God there is nothing to fear, not because nothing scary exists, but because God has promised to fight on our behalf. God is strong--unimaginably strong. And God will fight for you. He will make it right. He will bring retaliation on your behalf and make you victorious because HE is victorious. And when the battle against fear is over, you will not be fatigued, but you will be refreshed, because he is the one who fights it. You need only be still. Psalm 56:3 says, "When I am afraid, I put my trust in you." It takes trust in the one who is holding you in order to sit still. When fear arises over the unknowns of your life and future, trust THE ONE who IS holding you. He is everything he says that he is. He is Lord. He is Overcomer. He is faithful.

HUSBAND & WIFE, take a moment now to ask each other, "How can I pray for you today?" Then write down those three requests in the space provided below. After you've written the requests, read the prayers below and add your spouse's three requests to your prayer.

HUSBAND PRAYS FOR WIFE:

God, I pray that you would remove all fear from_____'s mind. Let her find rest in you. Let her see you clearly as the the God who fights for her, and let her identity be defined as one who fully trusts you, no matter how big the battle ahead may be. I also pray for...

1 _____

2 _____

3 _____

WIFE PRAYS FOR HUSBAND:

Mighty Father, fight for _____today. Crush his fears and all of those things that may cause him to fear. Let him see you fighting for him, and let the sight of it build him up. I pray that the more the enemy would try to impose fear on him the more fiercely you would fight on his behalf. I also pray for. . .

1 _____

2 _____

3 _____

fear

Husband & Wife, each take a turn reading the verse below out loud as a way of speaking blessing over your spouse.

"How good and pleasant it is when God's people dwell together in unity" Psalm 133:1.

{ DAY 6 }
UNITY

WIFE READS:

Picture the face of God--glorious and radiant over his creation. Now picture him pleased with you. The heart of God is filled with joy when you and I choose to live in unity with one another--when we make a choice to not allow differences, or toxic opinions and personalities to bring division in our spirits toward each other. Words are often the cause of discord. Discord (the etymology in Latin, discordare) means "reversal of heart" (dis + cor). It would be a tragedy for us as married couples to reverse our hearts away from the one we have been bonded to. The Word of God says that a man shall leave his father and mother and the two shall become one (Matt. 19:5). ONE. One mind. One heart. If a heart is divided, it cannot function anymore. To fight for unity is to fight for life.

When we are offended by our spouse or by a friend, it is easy to take up our right to be bitter; but bitterness kills. Bitterness causes a reversal of heart. The reason God is so pleased by the unity of his people is because this means we are one in purpose and greater things can be accomplished. If the enemy can cause disunity between husband and wife in even the smallest area, he is one step closer to drying up the productivity of that couple as a power house. Philippians 2:2 says, "Then make my joy complete by being like-minded, having the same love, being one in spirit and of one mind."

Unity must be fought for. When a harsh word is spoken, when misunderstanding inevitably makes its way into your home, do not allow it to take root. Fight for unity across the board. Be quick to forgive. Lay down your right to BE right, and let God win as you humble yourselves toward one another.

When you fight for unity in your marriage (and a fight it can certainly be) you will also begin to see your outside relationships begin to thrive. This doesn't mean that you will never disagree with another person, it simply means that you are onto the scheme of the enemy who means to reverse the inner workings of your heart--the very thing that gives you life, joy, and freedom. Start today with forgiveness. It is the key to protecting unity.

HUSBAND & WIFE, take a moment now to ask each other, "How can I pray for you today?" Then write down those three requests in the space provided below. After you've written the requests, read the prayers below and add your spouse's three requests to your prayer.

WIFE PRAYS FOR HUSBAND:

Lord, I pray for_____. Give him the willingness and courage to fight for unity in every facet of his life. Grant_____favor wherever he goes. Help the two of us in our marriage to be unified as we submit ourselves to you. Protect our marriage and show us how to win with unity each day. I also pray for . . .

1 _____

2 _____

3 _____

HUSBAND PRAYS FOR WIFE:

Jesus, I pray for _____. I ask that she would experience the goodness of unity in all her friendships and relationships. I pray that she would be full of your love, understanding, and joy for those around her. Bless her today. I also pray for. . .

1 _____

2 _____

3 _____

unity

Husband & Wife, each take a turn reading the verse below out loud as a way of speaking blessing over your spouse. Personalize the verse with your husband's or wife's name. Read it twice so that both names are read.

"Do not be anxious about anything, but in every situation, by prayer and petition, with thanksgiving, present your requests to God. And the peace of God, which transcends all understanding, will guard_____'s heart and [his/her] mind in Christ Jesus" Philippians 4:6-7.

{ DAY 7 PEACE }

HUSBAND READS:

Peace is generally regarded as a conditional feeling. We think that if our conflict was resolved, then we would have peace. We think that if we knew how our challenges were to be overcome, then we would have peace. But that is not how scripture talks about God's peace. His peace is a peace that transcends understanding. His peace does not depend on circumstances. When we give our needs and worries over to God, he exchanges them for divine peace.

This might seem like an imaginary peace--just a simulated feeling of what we would have if everything was worked out so that we could have the true peace. But that is not it at all. In fact, it is the reverse. God's peace is the real peace. If it were possible, in some perfect moment, to have all of your problems worked out, with no worries, no challenges, no problems, no fear, and no conflict--if that were possible, the peace that you would feel in that moment would only be a simulation of true peace. True peace comes only from God.

God does not require all of our problems to be solved in order to obtain his peace (which is good, because your world will never be completely free of problems). All he requires is that you, by prayer and petition, with thanksgiving, present your requests to him. And in return, he gives peace--true peace.

HUSBAND & WIFE, take a moment now to ask each other, "How can I pray for you today?" Then write down those three requests in the space provided below. After you've written the requests, read the prayers below and add your spouse's three requests to your prayer.

HUSBAND PRAYS FOR WIFE:

God, thank you that you offer us perfect peace. Be with_____today and give her your peace. In every fear, every challenge, every worry, and every conflict that she faces today, cover over it with your peace--the peace that transcends understanding--as we present our requests to you. Thank you for your power to overcome anything we could ever and will ever face. I also pray for . . .

1 _____

2 _____

3 _____

WIFE PRAYS FOR HUSBAND:

Mighty King, I pray that your peace would cover _____. No matter how the circumstances of his day pan out, let your peace be the final word in his heart and in his life. May the overwhelming reality of your peace fill him today. I also pray for . . .

1 _____

2 _____

3 _____

peace

Husband & Wife, each take a turn reading the verse below out loud as a way of speaking blessing over your spouse.

"Finally, brothers and sisters, whatever is true, whatever is noble, whatever is right, whatever is pure, whatever is lovely, whatever is admirable— if anything is excellent or praiseworthy—think about such things" Philippians 4:8.

{ DAY 8 }
THOUGHTS

WIFE READS:

It has always been the intention of God that your thoughts would be saturated with excellent and praiseworthy meditations. Our original design was that we would be drawn to purity and righteousness. Because of Jesus Christ and his victory over sin, we have been given the renewed gift to train our thoughts once again toward the loveliness of God. When the enemy tempts you to believe that your dark or wandering thoughts are simply a product of humanness, it is our right in Christ to rebuke the flesh and lead our thoughts back to a safe and spacious place. We are not bound by what the world offers us to meditate on. We are not cows impulsively chewing on the cud. Instead, as we look for God in our homes, in our marriages, in our work places, as we talk about his ability, his authority, and his truths, we train our thoughts to feast and be satisfied in the goodness of God.

You become the free-est version of yourself when your thought life is under the authority and light of Christ, yet shame would tell you to keep your thoughts hidden. In the presence of Christ, thoughts of rage are turned toward repentance. Thoughts of lust are rescued to purity. Thoughts of judgement are bent toward mercy. Thoughts of self-loathing are set free toward confidence in the Lord. Search your thoughts today and be relentless to chase their motives down. You don't have to live an anxious, fear-filled, shameful thought-life anymore. It is the gift of God for you to enjoy a mind that brings you strength, truth, humility, and life.

HUSBAND & WIFE, take a moment now to ask each other, "How can I pray for you today?" Then write down those three requests in the space provided below. After you've written the requests, read the prayers below and add your spouse's three requests to your prayer.

WIFE PRAYS FOR HUSBAND:

Lord, equip_____to have thoughts that are empowering, effective, and truth-filled. Give him clarity and leadership over his thoughts. I pray that everything that he spends mental energy on would be life giving, and direct him toward you. Thank you for rebuking shame in both of our lives as we submit our thoughts to you. I also pray for...

1 _____

2 _____

3 _____

HUSBAND PRAYS FOR WIFE:

Jesus, I lift up _____to you. I pray that you would encourage her with truth-filled thoughts that come from your Word. I pray that she would not be drained by worry, fear, or doubt, but that she would be full of faith as you lead her thoughts towards you. I also pray for...

1 _____

2 _____

3 _____

thoughts

Husband & Wife, each take a turn reading the verse below out loud as a way of speaking blessing over your spouse.

"A good man brings good things out of the good stored up in his heart, and an evil man brings evil things out of the evil stored up in his heart. For the mouth speaks what the heart is full of" Luke 6:45.

{ DAY 9 }
ATTITUDE

HUSBAND READS:

The condition of our lives is largely a result of our attitude. Chuck Swindoll said, "Attitude, to me, is more important than facts. It is more important than the past, than education, than money, than circumstances, than failures, than successes, than what other people think or say or do. It is more important than appearance, giftedness or skill. It will make or break a company...a church....a home."

But many struggle with their own attitude. The way they feel about life is not the way they wish they felt. How can we change our own attitudes?

Jesus said that the mouth will speak what the heart is full of. But in every heart there are both positive thoughts and negative. So which thoughts are going to win out? Simply put, the attitude that will win is the one you pay the most attention to, the one that you repeat the most often in your thoughts, and the one that you give the most air-time in your words.

So if you want your attitude to change, make the decision to change it. Speak life over your circumstances. Draw out the positive thoughts so that they win the argument over the negative.

HUSBAND & WIFE, take a moment now to ask each other, "How can I pray for you today?" Then write down those three requests in the space provided below. After you've written the requests, read the prayers below and add your spouse's three requests to your prayer.

HUSBAND PRAYS FOR WIFE:

Lord, I pray that the thoughts that come through most clearly in_____'s mind would be the thoughts that best serve to honor you and uplift her own situations. Let her attitude today reflect your heart. I also pray for . . .

1 _____

2 _____

3 _____

WIFE PRAYS FOR HUSBAND:

Heavenly Father, fill up _____today. Let your Holy Spirit fill him to overflowing with the fruit that comes from knowing you. Let his attitude be marked by thoughts of you, and give him supernatural ability to keep a godly attitude through difficult things. I also pray for . . .

1 _____

2 _____

3 _____

attitude

Husband & Wife, each take a turn reading the verse below out loud as a way of speaking blessing over your spouse. Personalize the verse with your husband's or wife's name. Read it twice so that both names are read.

" _____, give [the Lord] your heart, and let your eyes delight in [his] ways" Proverbs 23:26.

WIFE READS:

What an intriguing invitation to have your heart delighted, thrilled, and even captivated by God. The offer stands that when you give the Lord your whole heart--meaning your trust, your will, and your identity--he will give back to you the adventure of a lifetime. The more you release each burden to God, the more you will actively watch his miracles.

What if the descriptor of your life was that, "it was miraculous!" This IS what it is to God and what it could be to you as well. We know the saying, "Jesus take the wheel." But what if he really did? Would you question his course? Would you worry over the pit stops he brings you to? Our God is all-knowing, future-creating, unmistaken in all his ways. Our view of this life is so very limited. It would be a tragedy to play it safe with our made-from-dust hands clenching the wheel in careful control when perhaps the safe journey was never intended to be the best journey.

The Lord is wildly thrilled with your future in him. He knows every heartache and hope. He sees every divot and destination. He is inviting you to give him your whole heart today. What is weighing you down? What is causing you grief? Today as you pray, pray with faith that God can bring about a miracle. There is a song by Bethel music which says, "let go my soul and trust in him, the waves and wind still know his name." What is the name of your "wave" today? Is it an appointment, or a bill, or a relationship, or chore? Speak to that wave the name of Jesus and let him bring the calm and resolve you are hoping for. We are but dust. What power do we have outside of Christ?

HUSBAND & WIFE, take a moment now to ask each other, "How can I pray for you today?" Then write down those three requests in the space provided below. After you've written the requests, read the prayers below and add your spouse's three requests to your prayer.

WIFE PRAYS FOR HUSBAND:

Jesus, I bring_____'s needs before you today. You know every stress point. You know what is weighing on his heart. I pray that you would do as the scripture says and delight him today by your outstanding miracles. We wait patiently for your will to be done as you take control of the journey we are on. I also pray for . . .

1 _____

2 _____

3 _____

HUSBAND PRAYS FOR WIFE:

Lord, I pray that you would protect _____'s heart. Give her great hope knowing that you are in control. I pray that_____would see your miracles today. Give her a steady heart that belongs wholly to you. I also pray for. . .

1 _____

2 _____

3 _____

heart

Husband & Wife, each take a turn reading the verse below out loud as a way of speaking blessing over your spouse. Personalize the verse with your husband's or wife's name. Read it twice so that both names are read.

"This is what the LORD says to_____: 'Do not be afraid or discouraged because of this vast army. For the battle is not yours, but God's" 2 Chronicles 20:15b.

{ DAY 11 BATTLES }

HUSBAND READS:

Being a part of any competition--whether it is a contest, a sporting event, or a military battle--is filled with anxiety and stress. But if you already know that you are going to win before the competition begins, the stress and anxiety go away. If this were possible in a real-time battle, you would see the whole thing differently. You could see the battle without feeling anxious. You would be able to celebrate every win as it happened. You could marvel at your side's accomplishments. You could feel the joy of victory through every step of the conflict.

Those who trust in the Lord should be free to live their lives that way. He has shown us that, through Jesus, the battle over our lives is already won. Living under the saving grace of Jesus means that our lives are victorious. We still go out into the battle, but we do it knowing the end result. We can celebrate each win knowing that they are not isolated successes, but rather, part of a greater victory. We can look for all of the ways that God's mighty power is being demonstrated in and around our lives, not wondering if it is there, but being sure that he is at work. And we can carry the joy of victory even when we are still in the midst of the fight. The battle belongs to the Lord.

HUSBAND & WIFE, take a moment now to ask each other, "How can I pray for you today?" Then write down those three requests in the space provided below. After you've written the requests, read the prayers below and add your spouse's three requests to your prayer.

HUSBAND PRAYS FOR WIFE:

God, help_____to see how you are winning the battles in her life today. Let the joy of your victory be her song. Show us both how your miraculous power is being manifested in our lives, and help us to trust in your strength. I also pray for . . .

1 _____

2 _____

3 _____

WIFE PRAYS FOR HUSBAND:

Mighty King, thank you that you have already won on our behalf. Let _____be filled with the joy of victory over our battles. Let his heart celebrate you, and let the confidence that comes from seeing you win build his faith for greater and greater things. I also pray for . . .

1 _____

2 _____

3 _____

battles

Husband & Wife, each take a turn reading the verse below out loud as a way of speaking blessing over your spouse. Personalize the verse with your husband's or wife's name. Read it twice so that both names are read.

"But let_____[who takes] refuge in You rejoice; let [him/her] shout for joy forever. May You shelter [him/her], and may_____who loves Your name, boast about You" Psalm 5:11.

{ DAY 12
REFUGE }

WIFE READS:

What do you need shelter from today? What thought process, what fears, what worries, what overwhelming hurdle taunts your spirit? The Lord invites you to grab a hold of him—to hide behind the Almighty God—who silences the enemy with a glance of his glory. Can you imagine rejoicing in the midst of your financial, relational, or very real life struggle? Can you imagine shouting for joy and boasting? These things are impossible if we are responsible for fixing the problems ahead, but we aren't.

The Lord beckons us to turn our worried thoughts toward his ability. Are you worried that God does not see you standing in the midst of the sludge? Are you afraid that he does not hear your prayers? Are you wondering if God even cares about your future? Take heart today because He does! The Bible says that He is the God who sees. It says He is the God who hears. It says He is the God who cares. And God does not lie. 1 Samuel 15:29 says, "He who is the Glory of Israel does not lie or change his mind; for he is not a human being, that he should change his mind." The Lord has made up his mind to care for you when you call upon him. He has made up his mind to be your refuge when you take hold of him. He has made up his mind to walk with you through difficult times, and he will not leave, abandon, or deny his post.

Psalm 5:11 tells us to TAKE refuge in the Lord. When you sense the overwhelming reality of your inadequacy to change the circumstances ahead of you, hurry up and TAKE refuge in the Lord. When someone takes refuge from a storm, it is the structure that absorbs the hit for the one behind its walls. Let the Lord go before you today. Let his truth take hold of your thoughts. Let peace wash over you as you trust your Refuge today.

HUSBAND & WIFE, take a moment now to ask each other, "How can I pray for you today?" Then write down those three requests in the space provided below. After you've written the requests, read the prayers below and add your spouse's three requests to your prayer.

WIFE PRAYS FOR HUSBAND:

Lord, let _____ take refuge in you. Let his thoughts listen only to the truth of God. Keep the lies of the enemy far from his mind. I pray that_____would trust your love today and that you would bless our future. I also pray for...

1 _____

2 _____

3 _____

HUSBAND PRAYS FOR WIFE:

Jesus, thank you for being _____'s refuge and provider--even in places where I cannot be. Surround her with your security and love as she trusts in your name. Thank you for guarding her today. I also pray for ...

1 _____

2 _____

3 _____

refuge

Husband & Wife, each take a turn reading the verse below out loud as a way of speaking blessing over your spouse. Personalize the verse with your husband's or wife's name. Read it twice so that both names are read.

"And my God will meet all_____'s needs according to the riches of his glory in Christ Jesus" Philippians 4:19.

HUSBAND READS:

This promise from scripture says that God will meet all of your needs. Does he have the means to provide for your needs? Everything in Heaven and Earth belongs to him. Does he have the desire to provide for your needs? He created you cell by cell, and he loves you like a father loves his child. Does he know what your needs are? He is all-knowing, and he has told us that he listens closely to the prayers of his people.

Since God has unlimited resources, since he loves you like a parent loves a child, and since he knows every need you have, the questions that remain are: do you believe that he will meet your needs? Will you trust him? Will you ask him in faith? Will you be patient for his provision? Will you recognize that it is God alone who meets your needs, and give him proper thanks for it?

God provides. And he does not do it begrudgingly. He provides freely and joyfully, and to those who look to him for their provision, he blesses with lives of freedom and joy.

HUSBAND & WIFE, take a moment now to ask each other, "How can I pray for you today?" Then write down those three requests in the space provided below. After you've written the requests, read the prayers below and add your spouse's three requests to your prayer.

HUSBAND PRAYS FOR WIFE:

Lord, please provide for_____today. Be her provision in her emotional, material, physical, and spiritual needs. We acknowledge that you are able to provide, and that your love for us means you want to provide. I also pray for . . .

1 _____

2 _____

3 _____

WIFE PRAYS FOR HUSBAND:

Heavenly Father, thank you for always providing for us. Help_____to trust you for provision even when it seems unlikely or impossible. Teach us how to pray, and teach us how to trust you more. I also pray for . . .

1 _____

2 _____

3 _____

provision

Husband & Wife, each take a turn reading the verse below out loud as a way of speaking blessing over your spouse. Personalize the verse with your husband's or wife's name. Read it twice so that both names are read.

"Where there is no vision,_____will perish: but [when_____] keep[s] the law, happy is [he/she]" Proverbs 29:18 (KJV).

{ DAY 14
VISION }

WIFE READS:

When I think about vision, sometimes I imagine a CEO casting the vision for their company's future to a room full of navy blue suits--the kind of vision that would inspire them to work hard for their bonuses, to please their high-powered boss, and make the company great. But the company of God—if you can call it that—is already great. It is already complete. It is already established in its fullness.

You see, vision is NOT knowing what is going to happen tomorrow. That is fortune telling. Vision is NOT planning so well ahead of time that you eliminate any hazard this life might throw your way. The vision that the Lord wants to impart to us is in knowing where our future hope lies. It is in knowing that heaven is our reality, that Jesus is the fulfillment of the law, and that every day on this earth we get to abide in Him, and by Him, and through Him.

Vision sees clearly that to honor God is the most beneficial thing I could ever pursue. Vision recognizes that I don't need to know everything ahead of me, I just need to trust the one who does. Vision understands that "for me to live is Christ and to die is gain" (Philippians 1:21); that truly living consists of a life controlled by the Holy Spirit, and dying to my own agenda, my own will, my own motives, and my own goals will bring me more joy and satisfaction than any successful CEO could ever experience. In C.S. Lewis' *The Problem of Pain*, he explains that Hell is actually the ultimate prize to living for self and Heaven is the ultimate freedom from the bondage of our own ignorant, destructive desires. To keep the vision of who God is, of who we are in Christ, and to look to the hope of eternity, is to live with a perspective that will keep you from falling apart. We often say that God never promised happiness, but in Proverbs 29:18, it says we will be happy when we walk in God's ways and trust his leading.

HUSBAND & WIFE, take a moment now to ask each other, "How can I pray for you today?" Then write down those three requests in the space provided below. After you've written the requests, read the prayers below and add your spouse's three requests to your prayer.

WIFE PRAYS FOR HUSBAND:

Dear Lord, I pray that both _____ and I will hold onto the vision of eternity, that you would remind us today that you know all things. Help our eyes to be fixed on you. I pray that you would guide_____and allow all that he does to be blessed as he honors you. I pray also for . . .

1 _____

2 _____

3 _____

HUSBAND PRAYS FOR WIFE:

Jesus, I pray that you would give_____vision for the days ahead. Give her eternal perspective on all that she does. Give her the strength to follow your ways as she trusts you to direct her. I also pray for. . .

1 _____

2 _____

3 _____

vision

Husband & Wife, each take a turn reading the verse below out loud as a way of speaking blessing over your spouse. Personalize the verse with your husband's or wife's name. Read it twice so that both names are read.

"But if serving the LORD seems undesirable to you, then choose for yourselves this day whom you will serve...But as for _____ and [our] household, we will serve the LORD" Joshua 24:15.

{ DAY 15
FAMILY }

HUSBAND READS:

Family is the basecamp for life. More than school, church, work, or community gathering it is where we form who we are. Think about it. At school you may have learned to read, write, add, and subtract, but with your family at home you learned to walk, speak, eat, share, and love. Nearly everything about how you behave and who you are is a result of (or at least greatly influenced by) the home you grew up in.

It is common to focus on the differences between ourselves and our family members. When thinking about yourself and your own family, you may immediately say, "I am not like my father because..." or "My mother and I think so differently." But it is important to remember that we focus on differences because we take the things we have in common for granted. We are all a result of the family in which we grew up, even if you strive to change that.

As a husband and wife, you are leaders in your own family. Whether or not you have children at home, your words and actions determine the course of this family. The command in Joshua 24:15 is to choose whom you will serve, and to live it out in your home. Godly husbands and wives must choose to serve the Lord and defend that choice.

When it comes to leading in the family, the words that we speak are vastly overshadowed by our actions and the way we structure our lives. For example, the father who teaches healthy eating to his children teaches nothing if he himself eats only junk food. The mother who teaches cleanliness speaks in vain if she does not uphold the same standard. Our family watches what we do far more than they listen to our words. Who are you choosing to live for? Are you living for the Lord? How is that choice evident in your actions and priorities? How are you leading your family toward godliness?

HUSBAND & WIFE, take a moment now to ask each other, "How can I pray for you today?" Then write down those three requests in the space provided below. After you've written the requests, read the prayers below and add your spouse's three requests to your prayer.

HUSBAND PRAYS FOR WIFE:

Dear Lord, be with_____and me today and help us to lead our family well. Give us wisdom to know how to act, how to encourage, and what to cut out. In our shortcomings, we pray that you would fill the gaps, and allow our household to be one that fully honors you. I also pray for . . .

1 _____

2 _____

3 _____

WIFE PRAYS FOR HUSBAND:

God, thank you for blessing our home. Give_____and me the strength to stand strong against those things that would try to destroy our family. Come to our rescue when we are in trouble, and root out anything that would put our family in danger of not being fully devoted to you. I also pray for . . .

1 _____

2 _____

3 _____

family

Husband & Wife, each take a turn reading the verse below out loud as a way of speaking blessing over your spouse. Personalize the verse with your husband's or wife's name. Read it twice so that both names are read.

"Blessed is_____when [he/she] perseveres under trial; for once he/she has been approved, he/she will receive the crown of life which the Lord has promised to those who love him" James 1:12.

{ DAY 16 PERSEVERANCE }

WIFE READS:

God's got my back. What a relief this is when we are put under "trial" so to speak. I believe we are able to persevere through hardships because we know we're not alone. We persevere because we know that there is something greater to persevere for. God loves you. He is for you. He is with you. But this fallen world does bring trouble. It does bear sickness, loss, shame, and pain. When the scripture speaks of persevering under trial, it is speaking of the testing of our faith. But all trials and difficulties put our faith through the fire, whether it be financial crisis, marriage trouble, sickness, self-doubt, or sin. Each one of these could be crushing if your spirit is not allowing God to convict, redeem, bring forgiveness, help, or awaited healing.

No one wants to experience difficult times. And yet, when the Lord of all Heaven and Earth comes to comfort you in pain, when Jehovah Jireh miraculously provides, when the Holy Spirit brings you to your knees in repentance and sets you free from attitudes that have kept you bound and bitter, when The Great Judge has the final say, we will stand in awe of his goodness and say, "You were with me all along. I never would have known your power if I had not been in my weakest state."

2 Corinthians 12:9 says that, God's grace is sufficient for us, and that his power is made perfect in our weakness. When we allow Jesus to empower us to persevere, we are positioning ourselves to see God move. When we don't give up or take the easy way out, when we choose not to take a detour that seems faster to us, when we press through when our faith is being mocked, we are about to see the One (to whom we belong) come like a lion and protect the ones he loves. God is not without compassion. He is not without justice. He is not without mercy. He is here to comfort you, and to bring you peace that passes understanding. "And, after you have suffered for a

little while, the God of all grace who called you to his eternal glory in Christ will himself restore, confirm, strengthen, and establish you" 1 Peter 5:10. Be strong. Don't give up. Don't lean on your own understanding, but wait for God to bring you through.

HUSBAND & WIFE, take a moment now to ask each other, "How can I pray for you today?" Then write down those three requests in the space provided below. After you've written the requests, read the prayers below and add your spouse's three requests to your prayer.

WIFE PRAYS FOR HUSBAND:

Jesus, I pray that_____would have the ability to persevere through all the difficult things he is going through. Help_____to sense your nearness, your comfort, and your equipping. Give him the ability to stand with integrity in every decision. Strengthen_____'s faith through every trial, that he might be full of hope that you will redeem all things. I also pray for. . .

1 _____

2 _____

3 _____

HUSBAND PRAYS FOR WIFE:

Lord, I pray that you would supernaturally give_____the ability to persevere in both the little and big things. Give her energy to accomplish all that she needs to do. Fill her with your joy as she continues in difficult tasks. Bless her day with good things. I also pray for. . .

1 _____

2 _____

3 _____

perseverance

Husband & Wife, each take a turn reading the verse below out loud as a way of speaking blessing over your spouse. Personalize the verse with your husband's or wife's name. Read it twice so that both names are read.

"Now faith is confidence in what_____ hope[s] for and assurance about what_____do[es] not see" Hebrews 11:1.

{ DAY 17
FAITH }

HUSBAND READS:

We cannot live for Jesus without faith. Ephesians 2:8 says that we are saved by grace through faith. Hebrews 11:6 says that without faith it is impossible to please God. Our faith in God is what connects us to him.

But what is faith? Hebrews 11:1 says that faith is being confident of what we hope for and being assured of what we do not see. It has been said that the opposite of faith is not doubt, but, rather, the opposite of faith is certainty. If we see something with our eyes, then faith is not necessary. In fact, where there is absolute proof, faith has no place.

The life of faith means taking what is not yet fully seen, and even what we have questions about, and living it out with one-hundred percent of our hearts. When doubt creeps in, remember that doubt does not necessarily damage our faith. Doubt can actually build our faith. When we bring our questions to Jesus and seek his voice, our faith is strengthened. In Mark 9:24, when the father of the demon-possessed boy said to Jesus, "I do believe; help me overcome my unbelief," Jesus responded by performing a miracle in front of him.

In the animal world, a great picture of faith is the rhino. Rhinos have very limited vision. They can only see a few feet in front of them, but they run at speeds of up to thirty miles per hour. Do you have faith like that? Do you have faith in God to do what he asks you to do even though you cannot see the end result yet? Remember that without faith, it is impossible to please God.

HUSBAND & WIFE, take a moment now to ask each other, "How can I pray for you today?" Then write down those three requests in the space provided below. After you've written the requests, read the prayers below and add your spouse's three requests to your prayer.

HUSBAND PRAYS FOR WIFE:

Holy Spirit, thank you for being present with us. Encourage_____'s faith today. Let her feel your comfort, hear your guidance, and sense your presence going with her. Build her up in those places where her faith is weak. I also pray for . . .

1 _____

2 _____

3 _____

WIFE PRAYS FOR HUSBAND:

Dear Jesus, thank you for being patient with us. Let_____know you in an even closer way today as you deepen his faith. I pray that you would build him up so that you can use him to do mighty things for you. I also pray for . . .

1 _____

2 _____

3 _____

faith

Husband & Wife, each take a turn reading the verse below out loud as a way of speaking blessing over your spouse. Personalize the verse with your husband's or wife's name. Read it twice so that both names are read.

"Jesus said to them, 'I am the bread of life; [when_____] comes to me [he/she] will not hunger and [as_____] believes in me [he/she] will never thirst'" John 6:35.

{ DAY 18 }
(COMMUNION)

WIFE READS:

Hunger and thirst are results of the fall of man. When we are hungry and thirsty, we are reminded of our frailty and our inability to go without nourishment. But God is the ultimate source of sustenance for humankind. He feeds the spirit and brings life to the soul. If you never ate, you would certainly die. But God has spiritual food for us that satisfies long after a Snickers bar. When we take communion, we remember our need for God. We remember that there is but one source where all joy, and hope, and life come. When we partake of the bread and the wine--remembering that we were saved from our own destiny of death--we rejoice in our dependence upon Jesus. And yet, our society despises need. This world celebrates the independent, but scorns the one who is weak. The irony here lies on the other side of the cross where those needy and dependent are raised to life, while those self-reliant run out of self to rely on.

God honors those who recognize their dependence on Him. Who are you? Are you a man and woman in need of a Savior? The sooner this becomes the identity you relate with, the more often you will be free to testify about the goodness of God. Find some time this week to take communion with your spouse. Align your hearts together as a couple who is desperate for the saving grace of God. It is here that repentance, humility, and relief set you free to love one another as Christ first loved you.

Communion started as the yearly celebration of Passover when Jesus told his disciples to remember his sacrifice as they ate the bread and drank the wine. In the same way that Israel celebrated the sacrifice of the Passover lamb when the angel of death passed over their homes, so believers in Christ celebrate and remember his sacrifice of our sins when he died on the cross.

HUSBAND & WIFE, take a moment now to ask each other, "How can I pray for you today?" Then write down those three requests in the space provided below. After you've written the requests, read the prayers below and add your spouse's three requests to your prayer.

WIFE PRAYS FOR HUSBAND:

Lord, today I pray for us as a couple. Help us to recognize our deep need for you. We align our hearts together and forsake our former pride. Let all self-sufficiency in us fall to the ground as we remember your sacrifice that was undeserved yet gladly given. I also pray for _____ and the things that are on his heart . . .

1 _____

2 _____

3 _____

HUSBAND PRAYS FOR WIFE:

Lord, I pray for_____that her belief in you would grow stronger than ever before. Thank you for your sacrifice on the cross. Continue to bless_____with the knowledge of your presence. I pray also for . . .

1 _____

2 _____

3 _____

communion

Husband & Wife, each take a turn reading the verse below out loud as a way of speaking blessing over your spouse. Personalize the verse with your husband's or wife's name. Read it twice so that both names are read.

"_____, let us not love with words or speech, but with actions and in truth" 1 John 3:18.

{ DAY 19
LOVE }

HUSBAND READS:

You do not have to search very far in the Bible to find a passage about love. This virtue is mentioned over five-hundred times in scripture: God is love, love is the fruit of the Spirit, they will know we are Jesus' disciples by our love, love never fails...

C.S. Lewis, in *The Weight of Glory*, pointed out that if you were to ask twenty good people today, "What is the highest of the virtues?" a vast majority would say, "unselfishness," whereas the early Christians would said that the greatest virtue is love. There is a subtle, but important difference. Unselfishness is a negative feeling that we have to go without something. But love is a positive feeling—providing good things for others. Unselfishness is (ironically) self-focused. Love is others-focused.

Love means action. In our communities, our churches, and our marriages we are called to love—to take action. We are not just to speak love, but to show our love through the way we do real things for real people in the real world. Love in action is what should naturally follow from Jesus' saving work of grace in our lives.

HUSBAND & WIFE, take a moment now to ask each other, "How can I pray for you today?" Then write down those three requests in the space provided below. After you've written the requests, read the prayers below and add your spouse's three requests to your prayer.

HUSBAND PRAYS FOR WIFE:

Lord, I pray that you would inspire_____with your amazing love. Let her be so filled up with your love that it overflows from her as a natural expression. Give her divine appointments today that will allow her to express your love in a way that makes her feel not taken from, but given to. I also pray for . . .

1 _____

2 _____

3 _____

WIFE PRAYS FOR HUSBAND:

Jesus, you love us without limits. I pray that_____would have opportunities to show your love like a light that shines into darkness. Use us both to be a blessing to you as we demonstrate your love in our world. I also pray for . . .

1 _____

2 _____

3 _____

love

Husband & Wife, each take a turn reading the verse below out loud as a way of speaking blessing over your spouse. Personalize the verse with your husband's or wife's name. Read it twice so that both names are read.

"Who shall separate_____from the love of Christ? Shall tribulation, or distress, or persecution, or famine, or nakedness, or danger, or sword? As it is written, "For your sake we are being killed all the day long; we are regarded as sheep to be slaughtered." No, in all these things _____ [is] more than [a] conqueror through him who loved _____. For I am sure that neither death nor life, nor angels nor rulers, nor things present nor things to come, nor powers, nor height nor depth, nor anything else in all creation, will be able to separate_____from the love of God in Christ Jesus our Lord" Romans 8:35-39 (ESV).

{ DAY 20 }
HARDSHIP

WIFE READS:

Where's the love when hardship befalls us? Where is God when things fall apart? Is he causing pain or sickness? Is he removing his hand of blessing for spite? No. But hardship is the result of sin, and sin the reminder of how blessed we are to know a God who loved us enough to take it away. The love of God is always present when hardship comes knocking at your door. Difficult times will not defeat us if we allow the love of God to comfort our doubt. Hard times might take the wind out of your sails for a little while, or cause your heart to grieve. But in that tired tearful place, Jesus is present. "This High Priest of ours understands our weaknesses, for he faced all of the same testings we do, yet he did not sin" (Hebrews 4:15, NLT). Our scripture today does not say that hardship will never come, it says that love will never leave.

What hardship is ahead of you? Remember today the great love of God. His love is able to cover over confusion. His love is not afraid of questions. His love does not shy away from difficulty. His love never fails... and this, we all need to hear.

HUSBAND & WIFE, take a moment now to ask each other, "How can I pray for you today?" Then write down those three requests in the space provided below. After you've written the requests, read the prayers below and add your spouse's three requests to your prayer.

WIFE PRAYS FOR HUSBAND:

God, I pray for_____today that he would feel your love surrounding him when he faces hard times. I pray that you would comfort, provide, and protect him against the lies of the enemy that might cause him to doubt your love and goodness. Thank you for knowing our future. Thank you for using difficult seasons to make us into stronger people. I pray also for . . .

1 _____

2 _____

3 _____

HUSBAND PRAYS FOR WIFE:

Lord, thank you that nothing can separate_____from your love. Remind her that you are present in every circumstance today. I pray that when she goes through trials that she would sense your peace and presence. Give her a courageous heart to endure difficult times knowing that you are with her always. I pray also for. . .

1 _____

2 _____

3 _____

hardship

Husband & Wife, each take a turn reading the verse below out loud as a way of speaking blessing over your spouse. Personalize the verse with your husband's or wife's name. Read it twice so that both names are read.

"Be devoted to_____in love. Honor_____above yourself. Never be lacking in zeal, but keep your spiritual fervor, serving the Lord" Romans 12:10-11.

{ DAY 21 PASSION }

HUSBAND READS:

Passion, fervor, and zeal are words that should describe the Christian faith. The Good News about Jesus is awe-inspiring. It is passion-inducing. A life that understands who Jesus is and what he did for each one of us is a life that is filled with passion.

But it is not just our faith that should be passion-filled. Every part of our lives should be marked by fervor and zeal. Jesus said that he came so that we may have life and have it to the full. In everything—the way we work, the way we serve, the way we conduct our homes, and the way we live out our marriages—passion should come through.

And while Jesus does give us this passion as a gift, note what Romans 12:11 says. We are instructed to keep this zeal and fervor alive. It is our job to work at being zealous.

It is very likely that there are some areas of your life where you do not feel passion coming through. How can you tie those things into the passion that comes from Christ's love? What are the things that you are passionate about? Is it your job? Or a specific cause? Or a hobby? What is it about that thing that brings you enthusiasm? How can you cause that kind of zeal to come through in:

      -Your church?
      -Your family?
      -Your marriage?
      ...Or wherever passion is lacking.

God's desire is that his fervor would be present in every area of your life. Ask him to fill you with passion today.

HUSBAND & WIFE, take a moment now to ask each other, "How can I pray for you today?" Then write down those three requests in the space provided below. After you've written the requests, read the prayers below and add your spouse's three requests to your prayer.

HUSBAND PRAYS FOR WIFE:

Lord, fill_____with godly passion in every area of her life. I pray that she would feel refreshed and renewed as she goes throughout her day because of the new fervor that you build in her. May her whole day be marked with evidence of your goodness. I also pray for . . .

1 _____

2 _____

3 _____

WIFE PRAYS FOR HUSBAND:

Jesus, I pray that you would give_____a brighter vision than ever before of how you are working in his life. Let him find new things that build passion in him. Bring new passion to _____for the things that he need to do each day. I also pray for . . .

1 _____

2 _____

3 _____

passion

Husband & Wife, each take a turn reading the verse below out loud as a way of speaking blessing over your spouse.

"See to it that no one fails to obtain the grace of God; that no "root of bitterness" springs up and causes trouble, and by it many become defiled" Hebrews 12:15.

{ DAY 22 }
GRACE

WIFE READS:

The Lord wants good things for your marriage. It's his heart that you would grab a hold of grace, and that grace would thrive between the two of you. The enemy knows that if you begin to harbor bitterness toward your spouse, it will affect every area of your life and possibly jeopardize your future. We have to be vigilant at practicing grace toward one another. We have opportunities to extend grace each and every day: to our co-workers, our kids, our neighbors, even to other drivers on the road (that's the hardest one of all). Grace does not come naturally to the flesh. Our sinful nature wants to give people what they deserve, but Jesus models the opposite.

We describe the grace given to us by God as something that is undeserved, and that's exactly what grace is: undeserved pardon. But it's difficult to extend that kind of God-given grace to someone who has offended us, wronged us, spoken unkindly toward us, or even misunderstood us. The only way we can give grace to our spouse or to any other person is by continually acknowledging the grace of God in our own lives. God's grace to us covers every wrong thought, every wrong motive, and every self-serving right. If given over to our rights, we are condemned to death by our own sin. But given over to Christ, we are saved by grace. Ask the Lord to fill you with his grace for one another that you might thrive as you forgive and receive that same forgiveness and grace.

HUSBAND & WIFE, take a moment now to ask each other, "How can I pray for you today?" Then write down those three requests in the space provided below. After you've written the requests, read the prayers below and add your spouse's three requests to your prayer.

WIFE PRAYS FOR HUSBAND:

Dear Lord, I pray for_____that you would amaze him with your grace. Fill us both with grace for each other and for those around us today. Let our thoughts be acceptable in your sight as we humble ourselves before you, Holy God. I pray also for. . .

1 _____

2 _____

3 _____

HUSBAND PRAYS FOR WIFE:

Dear Lord, fill_____with your grace today for herself and for others. Let your Holy Spirit guide her thoughts and actions that she might be filled with joy because of it. Keep bitterness far from her heart by the power of your grace poured out to her. I pray also for . . .

1 _____

2 _____

3 _____

grace

Husband & Wife, each take a turn reading the verse below out loud as a way of speaking blessing over your spouse. Personalize the verse with your husband's or wife's name. Read it twice so that both names are read.

"Have I not commanded_____? Be strong and courageous. Do not be afraid; do not be discouraged, for the Lord your God will be with you wherever you go" Joshua 1:9.

{ DAY 23
DISCOURAGEMENT }

HUSBAND READS:

Discouragement is a deep feeling. It can be felt even when you are not consciously aware that it is there. Sometimes it comes on as the result of a specific failure. Other times there is no explanation for it at all. When it strikes, it can stay for just a moment, or it can linger for years. When you think it is gone, it has the ability to come back in an instant. And it can be debilitating. It can ruin jobs, relationships, and even self-worth. Discouragement can be an intense, yet silent destroyer of life.

But there is an antidote for discouragement's poison. That antidote is hope. Where there is hope, discouragement cannot last. Like light in a dark room, discouragement ceases to exist when hope takes its place.

The promise from Joshua 1:9 is that the Lord is with you wherever you go. That is a promise that brings hope! Where do you need hope to replace your discouragement today? What promise in scripture speaks to that need?

HUSBAND & WIFE, take a moment now to ask each other, "How can I pray for you today?" Then write down those three requests in the space provided below. After you've written the requests, read the prayers below and add your spouse's three requests to your prayer.

HUSBAND PRAYS FOR WIFE:

Heavenly Father, thank you for hope. I pray that hope would push out discouragement in every area of _____'s life today. Let places where she has been discouraged for months or even years be healed and set free as you pour your hope into her. I also pray for . . .

1 _____

2 _____

3 _____

WIFE PRAYS FOR HUSBAND:

Jesus, bless_____today. Let your hope win the victory in places where he may not have even realized that he had become discouraged. Build him up with everlasting strength that comes only from you. Let today be a new day. I also pray for . . .

1 _____

2 _____

3 _____

discouragement

Husband & Wife, each take a turn reading the verse below out loud as a way of speaking blessing over your spouse. Personalize the verse with your husband's or wife's name. Read it twice so that both names are read.

"Praise be to the God and Father of our Lord Jesus Christ, the Father of compassion and the God of all comfort, who comforts_____in all his/her troubles, so that_____can comfort those in any trouble with the comfort [he/she has] receive[d] from God" 2 Corinthians 1:3-4.

{ DAY 24 }
(COMFORT

WIFE READS:

What comes to mind when you think of comfort? A warm bowl of soup? A soft blanket? A friend by your side in a time of need? In our scripture today, God is given a title. He is called "The God of All Comfort." ALL comfort. This means that there is no lasting comfort outside of God that can meet the need that we truly carry in our heart, soul, and mind. It's so easy to turn to a quick fix when we need to be soothed. Yet, when we choose to comfort ourselves with something synthetic, we are denying God the right to be our comforter. He wants to function in that place in every area of your life.

When you have the opportunity to go and comfort a friend in need, you are not sent with your own wise words or ability to heal. You go with the Spirit of God which is working through you to bring his miraculous love.

To receive comfort, or to bring comfort is truly an act of God. Something far beyond our human comprehension happens when someone in need is comforted by God. It is like nothing else this world can offer. We can't bottle it up and take a sip of it when needed. We can't replicate it. It is like the peace that the Bible says "passes all understanding". The comfort God brings is not something that we can even explain, define, or put in a box. It comes as a gift as we allow the Lord to deposit his love in our time of need.

Do you need comfort today? The God of All Comfort is waiting to minister to you as you spend time in his presence. Is there someone who is relying on you to bring comfort? No need to lean on yourself to muster up some kind of magic touch. Instead, pray to the Lord and ask him to give the gift of comfort to the person who needs his miracle today.

HUSBAND & WIFE, take a moment now to ask each other, "How can I pray for you today?" Then write down those three requests in the space provided below. After you've written the requests, read the prayers below and add your spouse's three requests to your prayer.

WIFE PRAYS FOR HUSBAND:

Lord, I pray that_____would experience your miraculous comfort today. I pray that as he is guided by your Spirit that you would go before him and use his life to bring your compassion to those you put in his path. I pray also for...

1 _____

2 _____

3 _____

HUSBAND PRAYS FOR WIFE:

Jesus, thank you for putting_____in my life to be a comfort to me. I pray that she would also feel your comfort surrounding her today as she rests in you. Thank you for being trustworthy, Lord. Let peace reign in_____'s heart and mind today. I also pray for ...

1 _____

2 _____

3 _____

comfort

Husband & Wife, each take a turn reading the verse below out loud as a way of speaking blessing over your spouse. Personalize the verse with your husband's or wife's name. Read it twice so that both names are read.

"My dear_____, take note of this: Everyone should be quick to listen, slow to speak and slow to become angry" James 1:19.

{ DAY 25 }
LISTENING

HUSBAND READS:

If there is one thing that just about everyone needs to do more of, it is listening. Listening is so valuable, but so often ignored. In conversations, we may think we are listening when we are really busy in our own heads formulating the next thing we will say. In life, we fill our minds with distractions so that we won't have to be resigned to actually listening to what is going on around us.

Listening is precious. Listening shows you care about the person who is talking. Listening allows you to know them more deeply. Listening brings wisdom and insight. It inspires creativity, and even passion. And while it may seem undesirable or difficult to listen, the more you listen, the more you will want to listen. It is a gift to truly hear one another.

The place where we need to listen the most, though, is in prayer. When spending time with God, we are much more prone to talk than to listen. Think about how ridiculous it is for us to meet with the King of the Universe, but do all of the talking ourselves. God wants to speak to us, but in order to hear him we must quiet our own voice and take the time to listen.

HUSBAND & WIFE, take a moment now to ask each other, "How can I pray for you today?" Then write down those three requests in the space provided below. After you've written the requests, read the prayers below and add your spouse's three requests to your prayer.

HUSBAND PRAYS FOR WIFE:

Lord, help me to be a better listener for_____. Help me to hear her and know her more deeply. Develop patience in me to stop and listen for your voice as I read your Word, as well as through the voices of others, and through your Spirit speaking to me. I also pray for . . .

1 _____

2 _____

3 _____

WIFE PRAYS FOR HUSBAND:

Lord, help me to be a better listener for_____. Help me to hear what is important to him and to value his words. Let us develop a sense to hear your voice speaking and give us the courage to follow your instruction. I also pray for...

1 _____

2 _____

3 _____

listening

Husband & Wife, each take a turn reading the verse below out loud as a way of speaking blessing over your spouse. Personalize the verse with your husband's or wife's name. Read it twice so that both names are read.

"Create in_____a clean heart, O God, And renew a steadfast spirit within [him/her]" Psalm 51:10a.

{ DAY 26 }
RENEWAL

WIFE READS:

I love to repurpose furniture to bring it back to life or restore it to its former glory. And this is what God does with us everyday as we wake up and thank him for his new mercies. He loves to give us a clean heart. He longs to renew our weary spirits and to restore our souls.

But in order for something to be renewed, it must undergo a makeover process. It must willingly allow rough edges to be sanded, loose screws to be tightened, and fresh perspective to be given. Every morning we have the opportunity to allow Jesus to examine our hearts. We have the option to allow the Holy Spirit to sand away bitter places. We can let the Lord tighten our attitudes and strengthen our faith in him.

Psalm 139:23 says "Search me, God, and know my heart; test me and know my anxious thoughts." It seems odd that God would want to know our anxious thoughts. But as we share the things that are in our hearts (the good, the bad, and the ugly) we allow him to renew us, to clean us, and to lead us on his right path. It might seem a little painful at first to let God into the dark and shameful places of your heart and attitude, but as you allow him to renew you, you find new freedom to move forward by his grace.

HUSBAND & WIFE, take a moment now to ask each other, "How can I pray for you today?" Then write down those three requests in the space provided below. After you've written the requests, read the prayers below and add your spouse's three requests to your prayer.

WIFE PRAYS FOR HUSBAND:

Lord, I pray that you would renew_____today. Make his spirit steady and strong. Remind him of who he is in Christ and encourage his heart with those truths. I also pray for . . .

1 _____

2 _____

3 _____

HUSBAND PRAYS FOR WIFE:

Lord, I pray that_____would be cleansed today by the washing of your Word. I pray that her identity would be so rooted in Christ that she would feel light in her spirit and energetic in her heart. Thank you for your renewing power today. I pray also for . . .

1 _____

2 _____

3 _____

renewal

Husband & Wife, each take a turn reading the verse below out loud as a way of speaking blessing over your spouse. Personalize the verse with your husband's or wife's name. Read it twice so that both names are read.

"Yet the Lord longs to be gracious to_____... How gracious he will be when you cry for help! As soon as he hears, he will answer you" Isaiah 30:18a, 19b.

{ DAY 27 }
HELP

HUSBAND READS:

It can be difficult to ask for help. Most people enjoy the feeling of being self-sufficient. But refusing to reach out for help is not strength or independence. It is pride. Pride leads to destruction. And what is worse, pride is dishonoring to God.

When we neglect or refuse to bring our needs to God and ask him for help, our silent statement is, "I don't need God. I am better off figuring it out on my own than to allow him to intervene." This attitude is destructive--both to our relationship with God and to our own situation. We need his help.

That same prideful attitude is exhibited when we refuse to ask for help from others, or when we decline their help when it is offered to us. When we refuse to ask for help from our friends or our spouse it's like saying, "My dignity, my illusion of strength, or my reputation is too precious to sacrifice by humbling myself and asking for help." That attitude is the opposite of what God wants to grow in his people.

So what do you need help with? How can you practice being the kind of person that God wants you to be by giving up your pride and asking him, and others, for help?

HUSBAND & WIFE, take a moment now to ask each other, "How can I pray for you today?" Then write down those three requests in the space provided below. After you've written the requests, read the prayers below and add your spouse's three requests to your prayer.

HUSBAND PRAYS FOR WIFE:

Dear God, help us in those areas where we have been proud. Help_____and me to lay down our pride and look to you. I pray that you would open up our lives to the help of others, and let us be the kind of people who help and receive help easily. I also pray for . . .

1 _____

2 _____

3 _____

WIFE PRAYS FOR HUSBAND:

Lord, help_____and me to lay down our own strength and to rest on yours. Show us how you are helping us, and create opportunities for us to tell the wonderful stories of your miracles in our lives. I also pray for . . .

1 _____

2 _____

3 _____

help

Husband & Wife, each take a turn reading the verse below out loud as a way of speaking blessing over your spouse. Personalize the verse with your husband's or wife's name. Read it twice so that both names are read.

"Each of you should use whatever gift you have received to serve others, as faithful stewards of God's grace in its various forms" 1 Peter 4:10.

{ DAY 28 }
SERVING

WIFE READS:

When we serve one another, we are stewarding God's grace. God has given a measure of grace to each one of us, and serving others is the way that we exercise that gift. When you serve in your home, in your schools, in your neighborhood, at your job, or in your church, you are helping others experience grace so that they too might do the same for another.

Serving in your marriage allows grace to abound in a way unlike any other area of service. In essence, you are telling your husband or wife that you find joy in serving them because you get to reciprocate the grace given to you by God. Serving your spouse humbles your heart before the Lord and awakens you to his love and mercy. (And might I add, intimacy reaches its height when a man and wife serve one another well without expectation of return.)
Practice servanthood today. (Wink, wink.)

HUSBAND & WIFE, take a moment now to ask each other, "How can I pray for you today?" Then write down those three requests in the space provided below. After you've written the requests, read the prayers below and add your spouse's three requests to your prayer.

WIFE PRAYS FOR HUSBAND:

Jesus, thank you for putting _____ in my life. I pray that I would serve him well as you lead me, Lord. Fill_____ with a generous portion of your grace and anoint his hands for service. I also pray for . . .

1 _____

2 _____

3 _____

HUSBAND PRAYS FOR WIFE:

Jesus, I also thank you for allowing _____ to be in my life. I pray that I would serve her well as an act of love for you, My Savior. Bless _____ and fill her with your grace today. I pray that as she serves those around her that she would sense your pleasure. I also pray for. . .

1 _____

2 _____

3 _____

serving

Husband & Wife, each take a turn reading the verse below out loud as a way of speaking blessing over your spouse. Personalize the verse with your husband's or wife's name. Read it twice so that both names are read.

"Bear with_____and forgive_____... Forgive as the Lord forgave you" Colossians 3:13.

{ DAY 29 }
FORGIVENESS

HUSBAND READS:

Forgiving is one of the most difficult things we are asked to do in the Christian life. Jesus asks us to forgive others not just once, but an unlimited number of times. The reason that he gives as to why we should forgive is that he has first offered forgiveness to us.

To illustrate what a gift that is, Jesus told a parable, in Matthew 18, of a man who owed a very, very large debt to a king. In the story, Jesus says that the debt is the absolutely ridiculous sum of 200,000 years' wages. That is, conservatively, in the ballpark of five billion dollars by today's standards! This must have been astonishing (or comical) for the hearers of this parable. Who could ever incur a personal debt that large? But since the man could not pay the debt, the king simply forgave it. After the man left, he saw another man who owed him 100 days wages. But that man could not pay, so the first man had him thrown in prison until the debt could be paid. When the king heard what had happened he brought in the man whose debt had been forgiven, and had him thrown into prison until his debt could be paid. Jesus' lesson was that no matter how much someone sins against us, it is nothing compared to the way that we have sinned against God. He has forgiven us so much. He only asks that we follow his example.

In a marriage, there are many opportunities to forgive. When sinful people share life together, they will, at some point, do wrong against the other. It grieves God's heart when we sin against another person, but what grieves God's heart even more is when the person who was wronged refuses to forgive.

How do you need to ask for forgiveness today? And where do you need to forgive someone else?

HUSBAND & WIFE, take a moment now to ask each other, "How can I pray for you today?" Then write down those three requests in the space provided below. After you've written the requests, read the prayers below and add your spouse's three requests to your prayer.

HUSBAND PRAYS FOR WIFE:

Jesus, help me to forgive_____in the same way that you have forgiven me. Make me a person who forgives easily, and make me quick to ask others for forgiveness as well. And may your love be reflected in me in both situations. I also pray for . . .

1 _____

2 _____

3 _____

WIFE PRAYS FOR HUSBAND:

Jesus, help me to forgive_____in the same way that you have forgiven me. Soften_____'s heart so that it is pliable in your hands. Give him the strength to forgive and pour out your blessing upon him. I also pray for....

1 _____

2 _____

3 _____

forgiveness

Husband & Wife, each take a turn reading the verse below out loud as a way of speaking blessing over your spouse.

"Know that the Lord, he is God! It is he who made us, and we are his; we are his people, and the sheep of his pasture" Psalm 100:3.

{ DAY 30 }
BELONGING

WIFE READS:

"We belong to God." This statement can seem so elementary, can't it? But this is the single most important truth we can remember each day. Our minds, our words, our bodies, our identities belong to the Holy One. The Lord longs to protect and provide for those who actively stay near him and who listen to his voice--for those who identify as belonging to something far greater than themselves.

In 1 Corinthians 6:19-20 it says, "You are not your own; you were bought at a price." Even in our marriages, we belong first to Christ then to each other. When this truth is consistently at the forefront of our minds, it changes the way we live. Both husband and wife look to God for direction. Both answer to him in their attitudes and thoughts. Both understand that the Lord is the head of their home, and find great peace in knowing they belong to an awesome, very capable, God.

At times, worry about what the future holds can drive a wedge between you and your spouse unless you remind each other that your Owner also happens to be a miracle worker. Fear subsides when we trust in his ability. It's like the childhood song says, "Jesus loves me. This I know. For the Bible tells me so. Little ones to him belong. They are weak, but he is strong." No matter what your age, this truth will apply throughout your life.

HUSBAND & WIFE, take a moment now to ask each other, "How can I pray for you today?" Then write down those three requests in the space provided below. After you've written the requests, read the prayers below and add your spouse's three requests to your prayer.

WIFE PRAYS FOR HUSBAND:

Lord, I pray for_____today that the truth about belonging to you would reach deep into his spirit and change the way he views himself. Fill him with a holy pride in belonging to the King of Kings. Thank you that you have called him your own. I pray that he would live out today with a new perspective in his identity. I also pray for . . .

1 _____

2 _____

3 _____

HUSBAND PRAYS FOR WIFE:

Jesus, thank you for the gift of_____. I recognize today that she belongs to you, and I thank you for the opportunity to pray with her. Remind_____that she is yours, and that you are mindful of her. Bless_____'s day as she rejoices in her identity as your daughter. I pray also for. . .

1 _____

2 _____

3 _____

belonging

RECOUNT THE FAITHFULNESS OF GOD BY WRITING DOWN YOUR ANSWERED PRAYERS AS THEY ARISE.

NOW THAT YOUR 30 DAY PRAYER JOURNEY IS OVER
it's your turn to create your own personalized adventure.
If you have it in your heart to make praying together a habit, we would love to hear your story.
Feel free to email us at: lovingtheleapministries@gmail.com

answered
prayers

100% OF THE PROFITS FROM THE SALE OF THIS BOOK WILL GO DIRECTLY TO MISSIONS IN ETHIOPA.

The Myers served eight years (2004-2012) in Swaziland, Africa developing children's ministry. They trained children's workers throughout the nation, started children's camping programs and Christian Sports Coalition that became an effective evangelism and discipleship tool reaching thousands of children and youth.

In March 2012, the Myers sensed God shifting their focus to unreached people. Shortly thereafter, they moved to Addis Ababa, Ethiopia to work with the Assemblies of God church there to identify unreached people and to develop strategies for church planting among them. Since arriving to Addis Ababa, Ethiopia, the Myers have recognized the tremendous impact of urbanization and the need for a strong, vibrant, high-impact church there in the capital city. With a passion to reach their city and it's influencers, the Myers planted Eastridge Church Addis in April 2017.

YOU CAN
FIND ALL OF
REBEKAH'S
BOOKS ON
AMAZON.COM

{ ABOUT }
THE AUTHOR

Dan and Rebekah Metteer met at Northwest University in Kirkland, Washington and were married in December of 2000. They currently serve together as pastors in the greater Seattle area with their three children, Julia, Katie, and Andrew. Dan and Rebekah have a passion to see families and individuals grow deep in their obedience and love for Christ. They know that having Jesus at the center of every area gives the joy, hope, and adventure that each one of us long for.

Dan and Rebekah have been teaching on and about marriage for the last several years. Their prayer is that your marriage would begin to thrive as you allow Jesus into the very fiber of your relationships. They hope that praying together will be the springboard for healing and forward momentum in your married life.

Rebekah Metteer is also the founder of Loving the Leap Ministries. She has written several other books including *Faith, Friendship, & Focus*, and *The Fruit of Where I Dwell*. Her books can be found on Amazon.com. Every book produced by Loving the Leap Ministries goes to fund missions around the world.

**100% OF THE PROFITS FROM THE SALE OF THIS BOOK WILL
GO DIRECTLY TO FURTHER MINISTRY IN ETHIOPIA.**